# Junkers Ju 87

by
The Aeronautical Staff of Aero Publishers, Inc.
in Cooperation with

Heinz J. Nowarra

&

Edward T. Maloney, Curator of The Air Museum

Scale Drawings by Uwe Feist

*Aero Publishers, Inc.*
329 Aviation Road     Fallbrook, California

© AERO PUBLISHERS, INC.

1966

Library of Congress Catalog Card Number

66-22651

ISBN-0-8168-0528-8

All rights reserved. This book, or parts thereof, must not

be reproduced without permission of the publisher.

Printed and Published in the United States of America by Aero Publishers, Inc.

# THE JUNKERS JU 87 "STUKA"

The most widely used Stuka type, the Ju 87B-1 was the first introduced during the Polish Campaign of 1939.

Early Ju 87B-1 production model prepared for acceptance flight. Note extended Dive Brake.

# The STUKA's predecessor

The Junkers K 47 of 1928 was the Grandfather of the Stuka dive bomber. It was an extremely rugged aircraft and possessed excellent stability.

The Ju 87 V-1 was designed in 1934 and first flown in 1935. The twin fins and rudders developed tail flutter in the dive and the aircraft crashed.

Prototype mockup of the Ju 87 V-1 with the original twin rudder tail design as taken from the earlier Junkers K-47.

The second of two prototypes to be powered by the Jumo engine, the Ju 87 V-3 of 1936. In this model the twin rudders were replaced by a large angular fin and rudder.

Design prototype of the Stuka series, the Ju 87 V-1 employed a British Rolls Royce Kestrel V engine.

The Stuka production prototype, the Ju 87 V-4 (D-UBIP) had provisions for a single 7.9 m.m. MG-17 machine gun.

Junkers Ju 87 B-1 Stuka's under construction at the Junkers factory at Weserflug, Germany.

Close up view of Ju 87D dive brake. This Stuka was used at a training school hence the wing mounted 7.9 mm. wing gun has been removed.

Junkers Ju 87A first saw combat in Spain, later they were used on the Russian front in 1941. Note external bracing of the undercarriage.

Cockpit instrument panel of Ju 87B-1. Panel is well laid out with flight instruments set in the center. Throttle is at left, and pilot stick grip is offset to ease pilots hand fatigue.

Right hand view of the Ju 87 B cockpit. The handle marked "S" when pulled deploys the wing dive brakes. The large trim wheel is for elevator trim.

A large number of Ju 87B's were transferred to the Regia Aeronautica after Italy entered the war in 1940. The majority saw action against the British and Australians in the Western Desert.

Luftwaffe armor mechanics selecting 550 lb. Bombs for Stukas in preparation for sorties against French targets.

Luftwaffe mechanics pull through engine inertia starter crank in preparation to start Ju 87 B-2 Jumo engine.

Loading a 550 lb. Bomb under a shark nosed Ju 87 B-2 "Stuka" during the campaign in France 1940. Note mechanical jack to install bomb in correct position for attachment to aircraft.

Stuka pilots on wing catwalk prepares to leave office. Note rear gunners position.

Student Stuka Pilots learned the art of formation flying from veteran combat pilots. The men above are getting pre-flight instruction from flight instructor.

Stuka armor mechanic loads 7.9 m m. ammunition belt into the left wing MG-17 machine gun. Note 87 octane rating on fuselage side and Squadron insignia on front cowling.

Two mechanics make final adjustments on 550 lb. bomb attachments in preparation for sortie against Russian target. Note starter crank extending down from Jumo engine.

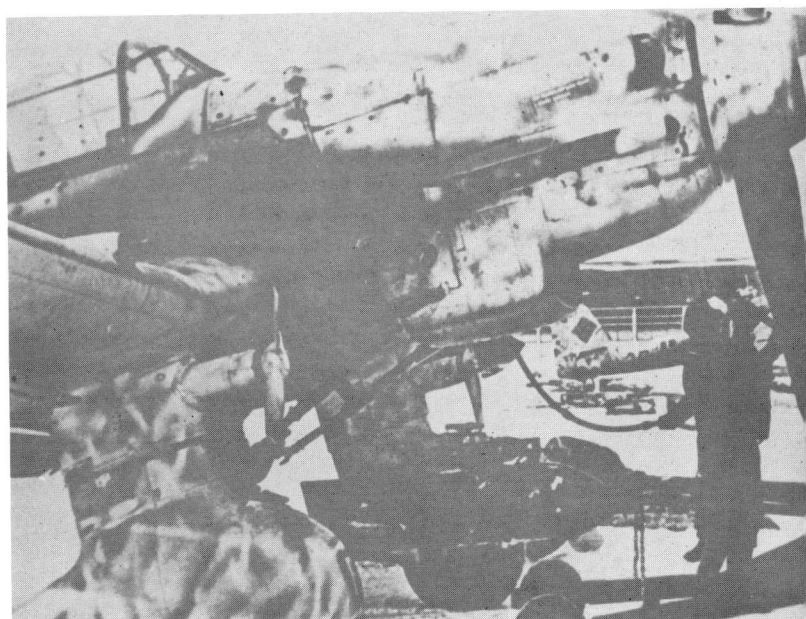

Junkers Ju 87 D-1 prepares to receive bomb load. Note unusual color scheme employed and two sirens on landing gear fairings, designed to create a psychological effect upon enemy.

Ju 87 B-2 closeup showing bomb in position under belly and 7.9 m m. MG-17 wing machine gun. Siren on landing gear fairing has been removed and capped off.

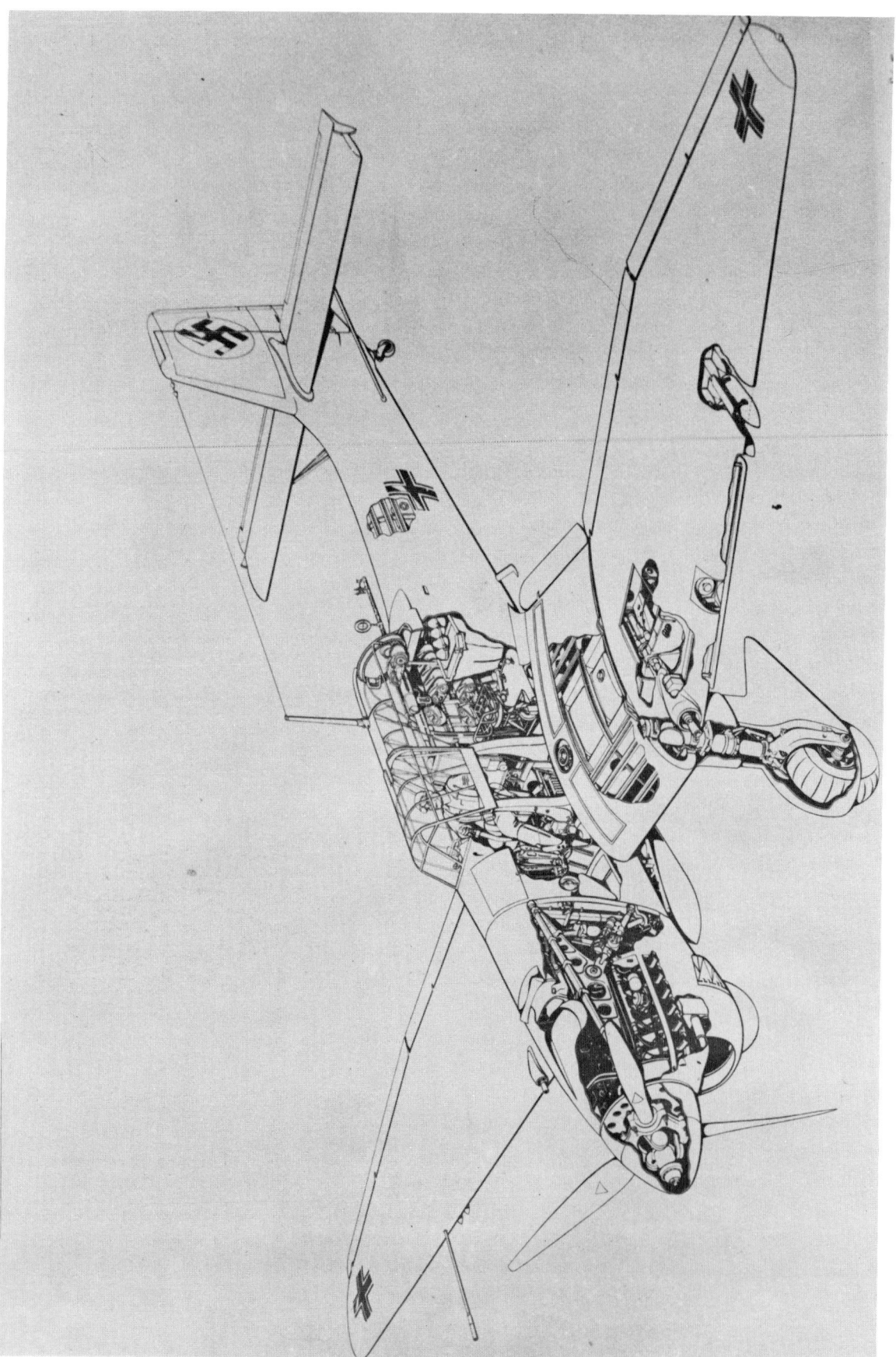

Cutaway view of Junkers Ju 87 B-1 showing wing and fuselage interior details. Note spacious two man crew cockpits, Jumo 211 engine and mounting, position of wing fuel tanks and machine guns.

A standard production Ju 87 B-1 is escorted to the Eastern Front by a friendly Messerschmitt Me 109E. The relative slow speed of the Stuka made it a sitting duck to any fighter.

The Ju 87 R-2 had provisions for external fuel tanks. It had a range of 875 miles and was used extensively in attacks against the island fortress of Malta, from bases in Sicily.

A flight of three Ju 87 B-1 Stuka's return from mission during the Greek Campaign in 1940.

Gagle of Ju 87 B-1's on their way home. Principal targets of the Stuka's were road crossings, bridges, harbor installations and ships.

String formation of Ju 87 B-1's in practice exercises over Germany in 1939.

# JUNKERS JU 87 A-2

JUNKERS Ju 87 A-2 in civil registration 1937.

# JUNKERS JU 87 R-2/TROP

JUNKERS Ju 87 R-2/Trop of the 3. Staffel Stukageschwader 1 as flown in Libya, 1942.

Scale: 1:72

Uwe Feist

JUNKERS JU 87 B-2 "STUKA"

JUNKERS Ju 87 B-2 of Major HANS ULRICH RUDEL cmd. of III. Gruppe Stuka Geschwader Z "Immmelmann" on the Eastern Front, Fall, 1943.

Scale: 1:72

Uwe Feist

# JUNKERS JU 87 D-3

JUNKERS Ju 87 D-3 in almost washed off winter camouflage especially applied with washable paint. This was used mainly to camouflage the planes against reconnaissance from the air, and also to make it difficult for a fast-flying fighter to spot a hedge-hopping Stuka against the winter landscape.

# JUNKERS JU 87 G-1 "CANNONBIRD"

JUNKERS Ju 87 G-1 "Kanonenvogel," of 10. (Tank) StG.1, with 2 X 37 mm Fla-Kanonen in special container under the wings. The divebrakes have been removed. Colonel Rudel flew a G-1 successfully against Soviet Tanks.

Scale: 1:72

Uwe Feist

Ju 87 B-2 with full bomb load in flight to the Russian Black Sea fortress of Sevastopol, the world's strongest fortification during WWII.

Ju 87 B-1 unloads its lethal destruction of one 550 lb. and four 110 lb. bombs.

The Ju 87 B had a cruising speed of 175 m.p.h. at 15,000 feet. The range with a 1,100 bomb load was 370 miles.

Three Ju 87 D-2's in formation over the Eastern Front.

In the first days of September 1939 during the Polish campaign these two Ju 87B aircraft were part of a force which attacked the Polish Naval Base at Hela, Poland. The first Stuka in pulling out of the dive hit the water and broke off both landing gear legs, but the sturdy built Ju 87B returned to base safely.

Mixed formation flight of Ju 87's on way to strike the Black Sea Fortress of Sebastopol.

Side View of Ju 87 B-2. The Stuka was very successful in the early campaigns through Poland, France and the Low Countries. During the Battle of Britain Stuka Units had to be withdrawn after six days, when air superiority could not be maintained by the Luftwaffe in attacks against Southern England.

Stuka trio — Pilot, Luftwaffe mechanic, and gunner pose beside Ju 87 B-2. Note relative large size of the Stuka aircraft to crewman.

Last production model in the Stuka series the Ju 87 G-1 featured a new redesigned wing. Used principally as an anti-tank aircraft in Russia from 1942-1945, the Stuka proved to be a most effective tank killer.

Ju 87 G-1 closeup. This model featured two 37 m m. Flak 18 cannon slung under each wing. This model had no dive flaps, and it was far from maneuverable, however, it was very successful against Russian Tanks.

Unusual View of the tank busting Ju 87 G-1. Note long extension of the two 37 m m. gun barrels. These cannons could not be jettisoned when escape from enemy fighters became desirable and this made the aircraft extremely vulnerable.

The Ju 87 G-1 as seen on the Eastern Front. It was especially designed to combat Russian Tanks, its rugged and sturdy construction saved many a pilot's life when he had to fly a badly damaged machine back to base.

Front View of Ju 87 G-1. Two 37 m m. cannons with wing-like cannon shell clips on each side of gun package give the viewer the impression of miniature missiles.

Junkers Ju 87 D-7 supplied to the Slovakian Air Force for service on the Eastern Front. The Ju 87 D-7 version had two wing-mounted 20 m.m. MG 151 cannon.

Luftwaffe mechanics prepare Ju 87 D-7 for mission. Bitter cold weather hampered Stuka operation in Russia. Field conditions during the cold winter months left much to be desired.

Flight of Ju 87 D-3's return from mission against Soviet strongpoints. The Ju 87 D series was extensively redesigned. It mounted the new powerful Jumo 211 engine of 1400 h.p.

Junkers Ju 87 D-5 in service on the Eastern Front. Undercarriage wheel spats have been removed to prevent frequent noseovers on the soft surface of the airfields. These aircraft have been pulled back under trees to avoid detection.

All bombed up and ready to go. These Junkers Ju 87 D-8 Stuka's are from Hans Ulrich Rudel's Stuka Unit. Note special long percussion detonators on the two outer 110 lb. wing bombs.

Adjusting of the two-wing MG prior to test flight.

Junkers Ju 87 D-I as captured in 1945 by American troops in a wood close to the Autobahn in Munich, Germany. Note special engine exhaust flame dampener installed for night missions.

Spring thaw on the Eastern Front was a muddy experience. Here a Stuka pilot poses in front of one of his Ju 87 D-5 which he flew. Undercarriage wheel spats have been removed due to field conditions. Note the installation of engine exhaust flame dampeners on his aircraft to enable him to attack Russian Tanks in the last hours of dusk.

Major Rudel flew 2530 operational missions and destroyed more than 500 Russian Tanks, the Battleship "Marat" and thousands of trucks, troopcarrier and armored vehicles. Declared as Russia's enemy No. 1, Stalin sent his best fighter pilots to hunt and ferret out this Stuka crew. Many didn't come back, but Rudel did, and now manages a Spa in West Germany.

Captain Rudel and his gunner and radio operator Sergeant Henschel. Rudel lost several gunner-radio operators due to Russian flak. He too was wounded many times but seemed to have a charmed life as he flew into heavy concentrations of Russian Tanks time and time again. The Russians always knew when Rudel was in the air by the large number of burning tanks dotting the steppe.

Artist's conception of Stuka scoring a direct hit on a Soviet T-34.

Captain Zemsky and his radio-gunner stand proudly posing in front of their Stuka after receiving the Knights Cross for stopping a Russian armored Spearhead.

Two T 34 lay burned out in a dry riverbed. Tanks in the background are German Mark III Tanks, far inferior to the heavier and better armed Russian T 34. The German Panther and Tiger Tanks appearing on the Russian Front in 1942/43 easily out gunned anything the Soviets could bring into action.

Ju 87 B-1 above gave way to the B-2 model which differed primarily in having larger propeller blades.

Stuka passes an abandoned Russian light Tank. Picture was taken from the rear gunner's position.

Western Desert Ju 87 B-1 (A5+L) in an unusual camouflage pattern.

Ju 87 B as found in Lybia by British Troops; below is a picture of the same plane after being repaired and given British markings.

Captured Italian Ju 87 B of the Regia Aeronautica. This aircraft was found intact by British forces near Tobruk.

An Italian Ju 87 B is examined by two British officers in the drive toward Tripoli.

Junkers Ju 87 B in later Italian markings.

Badly damaged Ju 87 B-1 crashlanded after attacking retreating French Forces in Western France. Part of the nose and the undercarriage are scattered over the field, note holes in rear Fuselage, probably from small arms fire.

Repairs to this Stuka in Libya were never finished. It had to be abandoned to advancing Australian Troops.

Ju 87 G-1 found scattered among other German aircraft on a Munich airfield in March 1945.

Junkers Ju 87 D-1 undergoing battle damage repair by Luftwaffe personnel somewhere in Russia. The low speed made the Stuka a favored target for the Heroes of the Soviet Union.

Lineup of Ju 87 D-1 Stuka's from the Immelmann Geschwader. The Ju 87D had a maximum speed of 255 m.p.h at 13,500 feet and a ceiling of 24,000 feet with a full bomb load.

Ju 87 B's in Spanish markings and flown by the Spaniards during World War II.

Two Ju 87 D-1 Stuka's returning from a mission on the Russian Front. The Stuka was used in Russia throughout the war for missions against Soviet targets.

Two close up views of the Ju 87 B wing dive brake in the normal flying position and the open position—ready for diving.

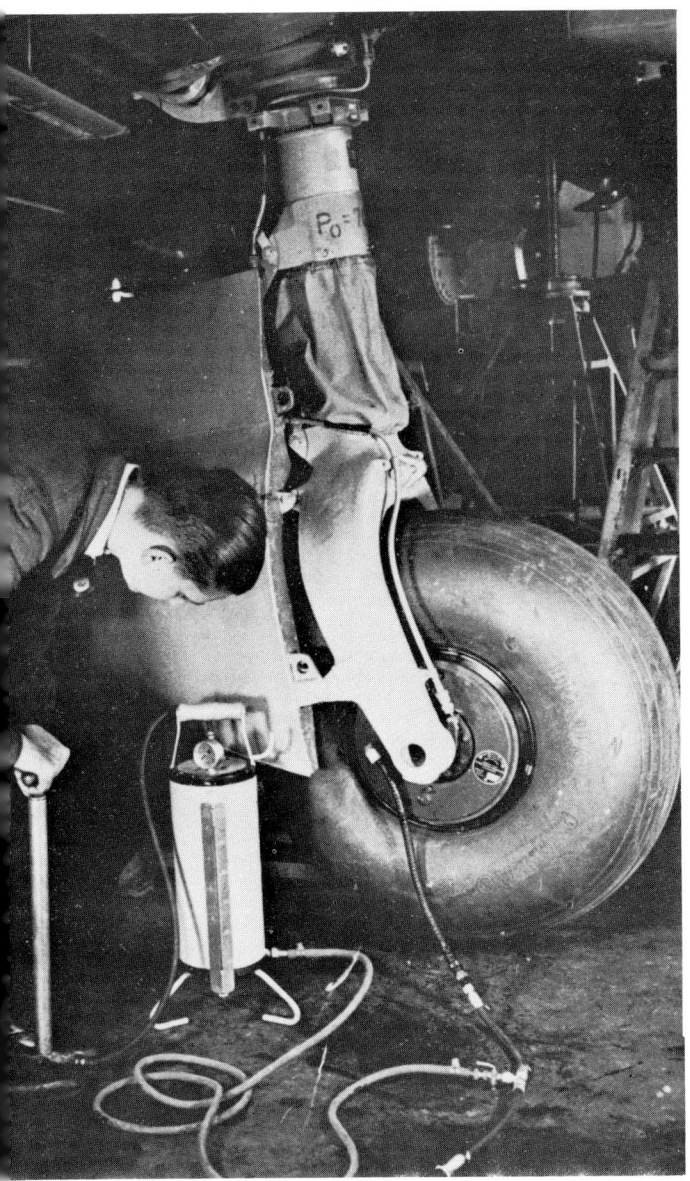

Close up view of the right hand landing gear. Mechanic is filling brake reservoir system. The front part of the landing gear fairing is removed. Note the large Dunlop tire.

Junkers' mechanic adjusting Ju 87 B engine. Note coolant radiator engine air intake.

Installing the Jumo 211 engine in the Ju 87B at the Junkers factory in Dessau, Germany. Note the rugged construction of the landing gear leg.

Two early production Ju 87 B-1's at the Dessau factory are awaiting the installation of the propeller. Notice the sturdy, light weight engine mount, coolant radiator, and oil cooler mounted atop the Jumo 211 engine.

Installing a new Jumo 211 engine in Ju 87 B. Four-point engine attachments made this a quick change unit, thus enabled mechanics to change Stuka engine in a matter of a few hours.

A 550 lb. bomb is attached to Ju 87B-1 Stuka central bomb rack by special hydraulic bomb dolly. Note how the bomb is held by bomb trapeze device which swings it out past propeller arc when bomb is dropped.

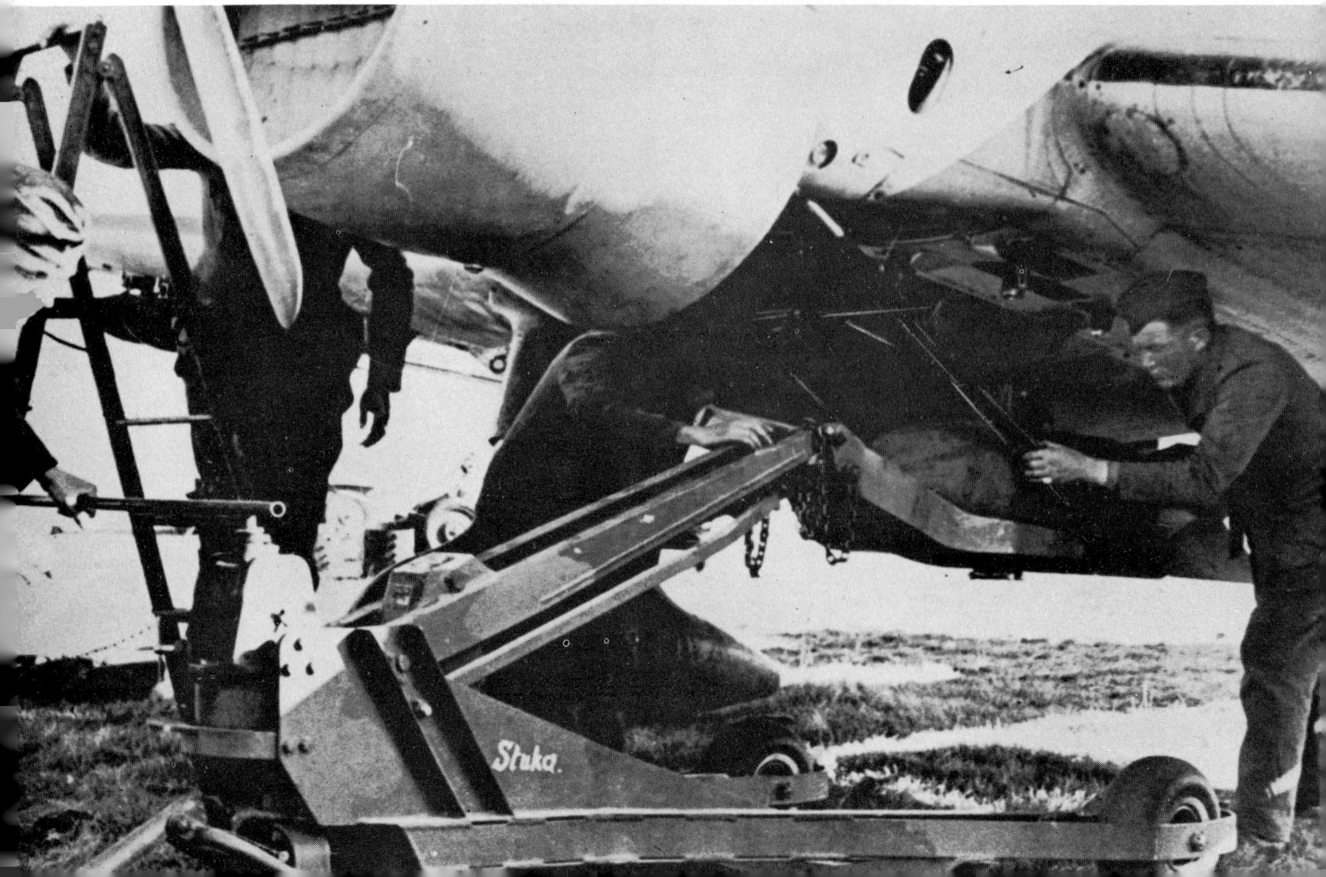

The large 550 lb. bomb of the Stuka was hinged to a trapeze so bomb would swing clear of propeller arc.

A Luftwaffmechanic makes final adjustments on a 550 lb. bomb before the Stuka takes off for another mission.

During the winter of 1941-42 a small number of Ju 87 B aircraft were equipped with ski's. This trial period did not work out satisfactory and so the aircraft were again equipped with conventional landing gear.

# THE JUNKERS JU 87 "STUKA"
## by R. S. HIRSCH

The vertical bomb run, otherwise known as dive-bombing, is not a new concept. Nor was it developed during W.W. II as often believed. Tactics of diving on a ground target and releasing bombs with precise timing were first practiced during W.W. I with widely varied results, ranging from poor to satisfactory. During the era between W.W. I and W.W. II it was found, through developing techniques and equipment, that pin-point accuracy with relatively small targets was possible with the dive-bombing approach. This was so because the biplane was still considered the optimum tactical weapon by designers. The terminal velocity was low enough for all bomb run aiming and pull out requirements. W.W. II was the first real proving ground for witnessing any over-all results of this method of bombing.

During the first two years of W.W. II, the JU87 was considered to be one of the most formidable and successful weapons of the German Luftwaffe. The demoralizing effect of the bombing attacks was further enhanced by the installation of a small propeller driven siren installed on the forward outside left strut of the landing gear, and requiring dive-bombing air speeds to function. These were called the "Trombone of Jericho" and, together with the howling effect of the Stuka in a dive, produced quite a psychological effect.

Col. Wolfram Von Richthofen was assigned as commander of the Technical Office of the Air Ministry, and he controlled the activities of the testing base at Leipzig. He had much to do with retarding the development of the dive-bomber type plane as a weapon. Ironically, he became the Commanding General of the Stuka-Corps in 1939. In 1936, Göring replaced Col. Von Richthofen with Ernst Udet as commander of the Technical Office and placed him as commander of a tactical unit. Since Udet, through flying at National Air Shows in the U.S.A., had observed dive-bombing demonstrations, the development of requirements was inevitable. It was through the urging of Ernst Udet to Hitler's scientific technical staff, known as the Fo-Fu, and repeated dive-bombing demonstrations by Udet for the General Staff and Luftwaffe high command, that a decision was made to create a plane for this specific purpose. Udet used a Focke-Wulf FW56 for these demonstrations.

Competitive contracts for development were issued and the development race was on. There evolved only four manufacturers who received initial plane development contracts. They were: Arado, Blohm & Voss, Heinkel, and Junkers. Arado developed the AR81. Blohm & Voss presented the HA137. Heinkel produced the HE118, which was developed by the Gonter brothers. Junkers presented the model JU87 developed by Dr. Pohlmann and Karl Plauth, who had designed the K47.

The AR81 was a biplane and was not sufficiently stable to warrant production or further development. The HA137 was a single-seater, and, as the program progressed, the General Staff turned toward a two-seater as the optimum concept for this type of weapon. The He118 was the most modern looking design, but the JU87 demonstrated superior stability and compactness of design which was considered desirable for this type of weapon. So it was chosen for all out development.

The wooden mock-up, first presented, had a bent inverted gull type wing taken from the JU52. It also had a double (twin) tail, almost identical to the K47. The mock-up was used in wind tunnel tests at Dessau and the first flyable aircraft was designated the JU87V-1. It was powered by a Rolls Royce "Kestrel" and was externally almost identical to the mock-up, except that the vertical rudders were now square instead of oval. The undercarriage was of a fixed gear spats type similar to the Northrop planes of that era. The bombs were still similar to those of the horizontal bombers with underwing bombs. There was a single rearward-firing movable gun enplacement with an M-15 gun. Two forward-firing guns, also M-15, were placed high and fired over the engine.

The JU87V-1 underwent the first flight testing in 1937. These brought about modifications which were incorporated in the JU87V-2. The JU87V-3 was the same as the V-2 except that it incorporated a JUMO 210C of 640 H.P. and a three-blade propeller. The JU87V-4, also designated D-U31P, first incorporated the dive-bombing bomb release fork. This carried the main bomb under the fuselage and swung it clear of the propeller arc. There was also an automatic pullout device which was activated by the bomb releasing mechanism.

All these "V" series were prototypes. Many of the experimental flights were made by a woman test pilot, a Flt. Capt. Melitta Schiller.

The JU87A-1 was the first of the serial production models, which began in 1937. The first three production planes went into service-testing in the Spanish Civil War. The following production models were delivered to the Luftwaffe. The Immelmann Sturzkampfgeschwader (Dive-bomber Group) received the planes and named them the Stuzkampfglugzeug" and abbreviated them "STUKA." Data from the Spanish Civil War and Luftwaffe indicated the JU87A was underpowered.

A JU87B-1 & 2 was developed by Dr. Pohlmann, which was his last works for Junkers. He then left Junkers to become chief of the design office for Blohm & Voss. All further JU87 development was done by the Weserflug EMBH, a subsidiary of the Deschimag enterprises which was a part of the Krupp-Works. The B-1 and B-2 differed only by internal equipment. Both models were powered by a JUMO 211-Da of 1210 H.P. Armament was changed to two MG 17's firing forward and retaining the single M-15 rearward gun. The standard bomb load was one 562 lb. bomb on the fuselage rack, and two 55 lb. bombs under each wing. Dimensions were the same as the -A series. Landing speed was 67.1 m.p.h. An altitude of 3,280 ft. could be reached in two minutes.

The JU87C (also designated JU87T, "T" for Träger) was planned and was to be a carrier operations version for use with the carrier "Graf Zepplin" under construction at that time. This work was stopped shortly after the Fall of 1939. Then, later in 1940, a JU87B-1 was modified into a C-1 by equipping it with an arrester hook, foldable wings, and a jettisonable undercarriage. All work on this version was cancelled in mid-1941.

The JU87D-1 was a development of experience in combat and test data. It had a JUMO 211J of 1300 h.p. The large forward fuselage radiator was removed and replaced by two smaller radiators under the inner wing panels. The oil cooler was kept under the engine. The cockpit hood was redesigned and more streamlined. The bomb rack was redesigned to hold a maximum weight of 3,969 lbs. The D versions were used extensively in the Balkans as a ground support weapon. There were two MG 17's wing-mounted guns firing forward, and a twin MG 18Z rearward firing set up. It could reach an altitude of 14,760 ft. in 19 minutes and landed at 68.35 m.p.h.

The JU87D-2 was the same as the D-1 with the exception of a single modification of a cargo glider towing installation.

The JU87D-3 differed in having a heavier armament made for ground strafing missions.

The JU87D-4 had a wing-installed WB-81 weapons container under each wing instead of bomb racks. This was nicknamed the "watering can" and housed six MG 81's, four firing forward and two backwards for firing during pullout and climb.

The JU87D-5 was extensively modified. It sported a new wing with large span and modification of the air-brakes automatic pullout device. This was to achieve higher diving speeds made necessary by the steadily growing anti-aicraft firepower. It also incorporated a jettisonable undercarriage for emergency field operations.

The JU87D-6 remains unknown. It is possible that none were built, since records or photo identification are unobtainable.

The JU87D-7 retained the wing of the D-5, but had a 20 mm. MG-151/20 gun package under each wing. This was used as an anti-tank weapon on the Eastern Front. A single MG 81Z was the remaining armament. Capt. Rudel became the leading ace in anti-tank analysis. The MG-151/20 guns were still too light and too low a muzzle velocity for the T-34 tanks; and Capt. Rudel kept asking for a heavier gun. The Technical Office of the Air Ministry assigned a JU87D-3 for tests, and a Fluk 18 of 3.7cm gun was selected for wing installation. It used anti-tank tracer shells and developed a muzzle velocity of 2158.9 ft. per sec. Extensive modifications and development were undertaken to stabilize the guns and to make the wing structure withstand the recoil. Capt. Rudel flew the test mission on a captured T-34, and his dive was almost vertical. The shell penetrated the roof and exploded inside, completely destroying the tank.

The JU87G-1 was the outcome of Capt. Rudel's tests. He selected two first line JU87 pilots and set out to demonstrate the ability of his new weapon. His success is well known, and this became a new breath of life for the now aging JU87 Stuka weapon. It has been often stated that Rudel alone, had destroyed enough tanks to equip a complete armored division.

There were only two more models produced. They were the JU87H and JU87R. The JU87H was a rebuilt JU87D-1, used for training purposes. It had dual controls and the rear armament removed. The JU87R was a modified B-1 series. The "R" stands for "Reichweite" or range. The outer wing racks were modified to carry a 300 liter (79.2 U. S. gals.) external tank. The metal tanks in the wings were also replaced by fabric ones which would expand outward into the wing crevices and thereby contained an increased fuel capacity. Range was increased to 932.1 miles. This version was used in Africa, on Malta raids and on general Italian campaigns.

Outside of the American Douglas Dauntless, the Stuka enjoyed the distinction of being the only mass produced dive bomber of W.W. II. The JU87 was unique and although obsolete within two years after the beginning of W.W. II, went on to see action almost all through the war.

A. Junkers Ju 87 B-2/Trop as it is on display today in the Museum of Science and Industry, Chicago, Illinois.

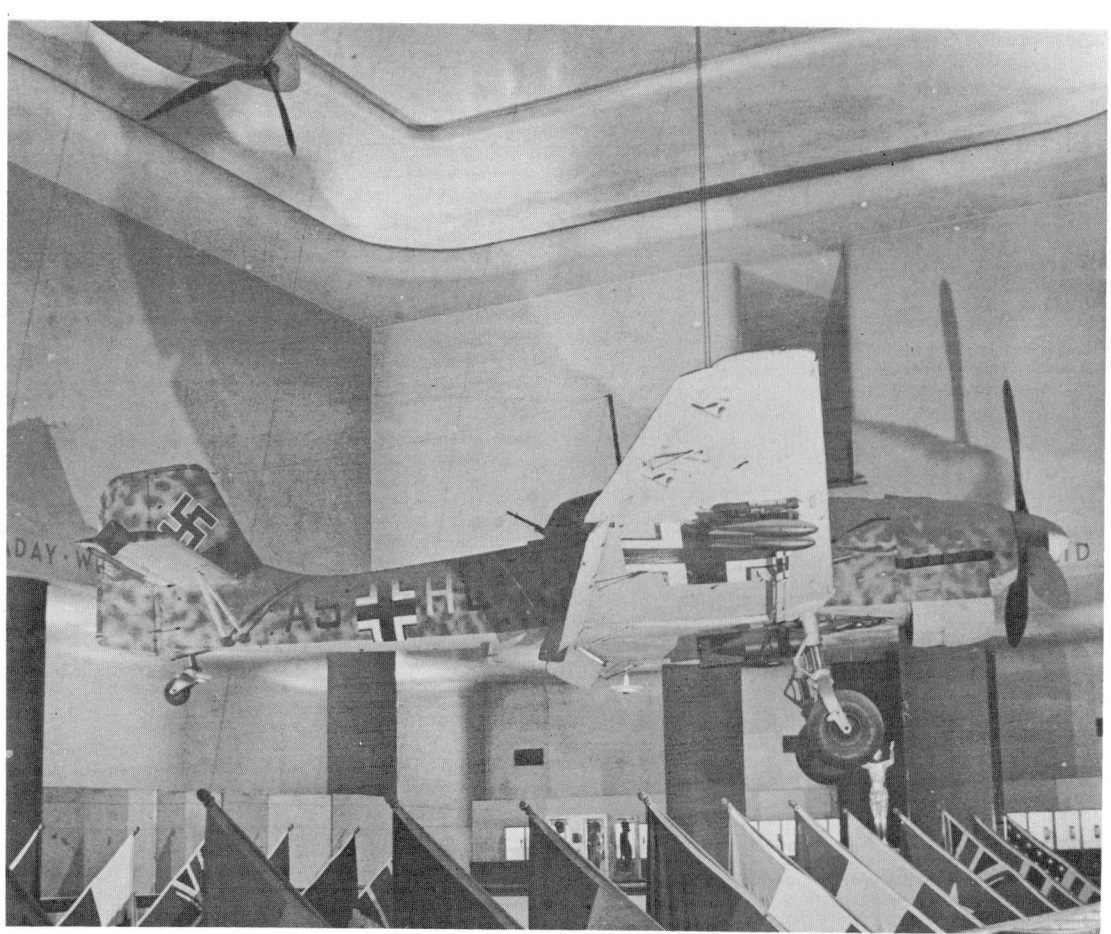

Ju 87 B of the 7. Staffel, Stukageschwader 77.

Ju 87 B's of StG2 with Palm Eagle and Swastika on the motor cowling on a mission over Libya.

| Model | Span ft. | Length ft. | Height ft. | Wing Area sq. ft. | Wt. Empty lbs. | Gross Wt. lbs. | Range miles | Max. Speed mph | Cruise Speed mph | Service Ceiling ft. |
|---|---|---|---|---|---|---|---|---|---|---|
| JU87 A | 45.26 | 35.42 | 12.73 | 344.32 | 5,005.35 | 7,497 | 621.4 | 198.85 | 174 | 22,960 |
| JU87 B | 45.26 | 35.42 | 12.73 | 344.32 | 6,088.8 | 9,562.5 | 497.1 | 240.48 | 211.3 | 26,568 |
| JU87 C | 45.26 | 35.42 | 12.73 | 344.32 | 6,408 | 9,952 | Unknown | 235 | 211.3 | Unknown |
| JU87 D (D-1 thru D-4) | 45.26 | 35.42 | 12.73 | 344.32 | Unknown | 12,650 | 621.4 | 253.5 | 229.9 | 24,030 |
| JU87 D-5 | 49.2 | 35.42 | 12.73 | 362.6 | Unknown | 14,230 | Unknown | Unknown | Unknown | Unknown |
| JU87 D-7 | 49.2 | 35.42 | 12.73 | 362.6 | Unknown | 14,545 | 1,193.4 | 248.56 @ 15,432 ft. | Unknown | 24,600 |
| JU87 G | 49.2 | 35.42 | 12.73 | 362.6 | Unknown | 14,540 | 1,250 | 250 | Unknown | 24,600 |
| JU87 R | 45.26 | 35.42 | 12.73 | 344.32 | 6,200 | 12,600 | 932.1 | 235 | 211 | 23,900 |
| JU87 H | 45.26 | 35.42 | 12.73 | 344.32 | Unknown | 11,450 | 621.4 | 255.5 | 230 | 26,600 |

Experimental Ju 87 D modified to carry wounded personnel from battlefront to rear area.

Junkers Ju 87 B modified to carry wing foil shape container to carry urgently needed supplies to forward areas.

Ju 87 D-2 of 1./St. G.1 bombed up and ready for another sortie against Soviet troop concentrations, note special anti-personnel bombs under the wings.

# Aero Shop

by AL PARKER

## JUNKERS JU 87

Recently a friend asked, "Al, where can I find a good model of the Stuka dive bomber? Of all the World War II planes, that bent wing beast intrigues me the most." His sentiment seems to hold true for a good many modelers — possibly because of the stories that were told of it during its heyday. Nevertheless the Ju87 is an intriguing aircraft and should be part of your collection.

As for an answer to my friend's question, this was simple. The recently released Imai Ju 87 B-I from Japan in 1:50 scale is probably the best example of this plane. Recent Japanese kits generally seem to be of good quality and this kit is no exception. Detail is very good with only minor flash removal and clean up necessary. Rivets and panel lines are a bit heavy, but are still within the limits of acceptability. The only rivets we would recommend removing are those on the wheel pants. The pattern is completely wrong, and then too the pants should be filled with body putty and reshaped as those furnished are too flat. The only other possible criticism rests in the four-piece canopy. To the serious builder the canopy will appear to be too thick. However, if left in the open position — this isn't too noticeable. Aside from these two items, with normal seam and joint filling, the kit builds into a very presentable model. For those of you who like gimmicks, the Imai kit has a trigger on the right side of the fuselage to release the bomb should you care to display your prowess in hangar flying.

The sister kit to the Imai model, scale wise, is the Lindberg Ju 87 B-I. Being the "Granddaddy" of all plastic Stukas, this kit suffers from a few inaccuracies, but all in all runs a very close second to Imai. The one glaring error in the Lindberg model is the width of the chord at the wing tip, approximately twice what it should be.

For the 1:72 scale enthusiast, Airfix also has a Ju 87 B-I. General outline and scale are very good and because of greatly reduced detail the kit is quite simple to assemble. There are no rivets on this model to be concerned with. Panel lines are heavy and will need a little sanding down. Seam and joint lines are also a bit rough and filling in with body putty is a must.

Unfortunately, the only model company with enough forethought to release a different mark Stuka did so in a scale almost too small to bother with. Faller's Ju 87 G-I in 1:100 scale is complete with twin 37 mm wing cannons and an excellent decal sheet. Other Stukas in this scale range are UPC's Ju 87 B in 1:100 and the now unobtainable Eagle Ju 87 B in 1:96.

To convert a Ju 87 B-I into a Ju 87 G-I, cement the fuselage halves together, cut the entire engine off immediately in front of the wing leading edge. This discarded engine can now be used as a rough template for the new engine you will have to carve. Note! The new engine must be 1½ scale feet longer than the original. Refer to the profiles here in Aero Series for the correct proportions. After the new nose has been fitted to the fuselage, add a dorsal fillet to the vertical fin, new one-piece struts to the elevators, and a new air scoop to the right side of the nose six scale inches behind the spinner. The following step pertains only to those modifying the Lindberg kit. Do not use the wings furnished in the kit, rather, obtain a wing from an Imai kit. Cement them together, cut out the center section and mate these to the fuselage of the Lindberg kit. A small amount of wing root filling and sanding will be required, but the resultant model will be much more accurate.

Next, the modeler must choose which type of landing gear to use, full panted or partially exposed strut and wheel. Both were used on the G-I and it is our opinion that mud packing into the wheel cavities caused mechanics to remove the "pants" during wet weather operations. Should you elect to use the exposed type, cut the furnished landing gear off immediately below the large section of the panted strut. From your parts file, select a "tuning fork" strut that fits the furnished wheel, drill a hole in the stub fairing to receive this new strut, and assemble. Note: If the new strut does not have a torque link on the rear side, this should be added.

The two 37mm cannons can be made from the following items: gun housings from Japanese type external fuel tanks, gun barrels from discarded tank kits (less muzzles, these must be turned from scrap plastic), gun support fairings and ammo trays from flat scrap plastic. Again refer to the profile here in Aero Series for the correct sizes.

As you may have begun to see, a surplus parts file is a conversionist's best friend.

The G-l did not have dive brakes, so these should be omitted and the gun ports in the leading edge of the wing should be filled in.

Probably the most difficult item to make for those of us who do not have lathes, is a propeller spinner. The G-l spinner was quite different from the B-l and hence requires reworking. Starting with a spinner from a Hawker Hurricane kit, fit the Stuka prop to it. (If the Monogram spinner is used, the spinner and blades are one piece and need only slight reshaping to be satisfactory.) Next add a plastic disc to the rear of the spinner approximately six scale inches thick. Finish smooth and mount.

As a finishing touch to your modified G-l, add counterweights to the outboard ailerons (2 each). These may be obtained from Hawk V-l or Baka Bomb kits.

Stuka pilot proudly displays his belt on which he marked every mission he flew during the early months of the French campaign.

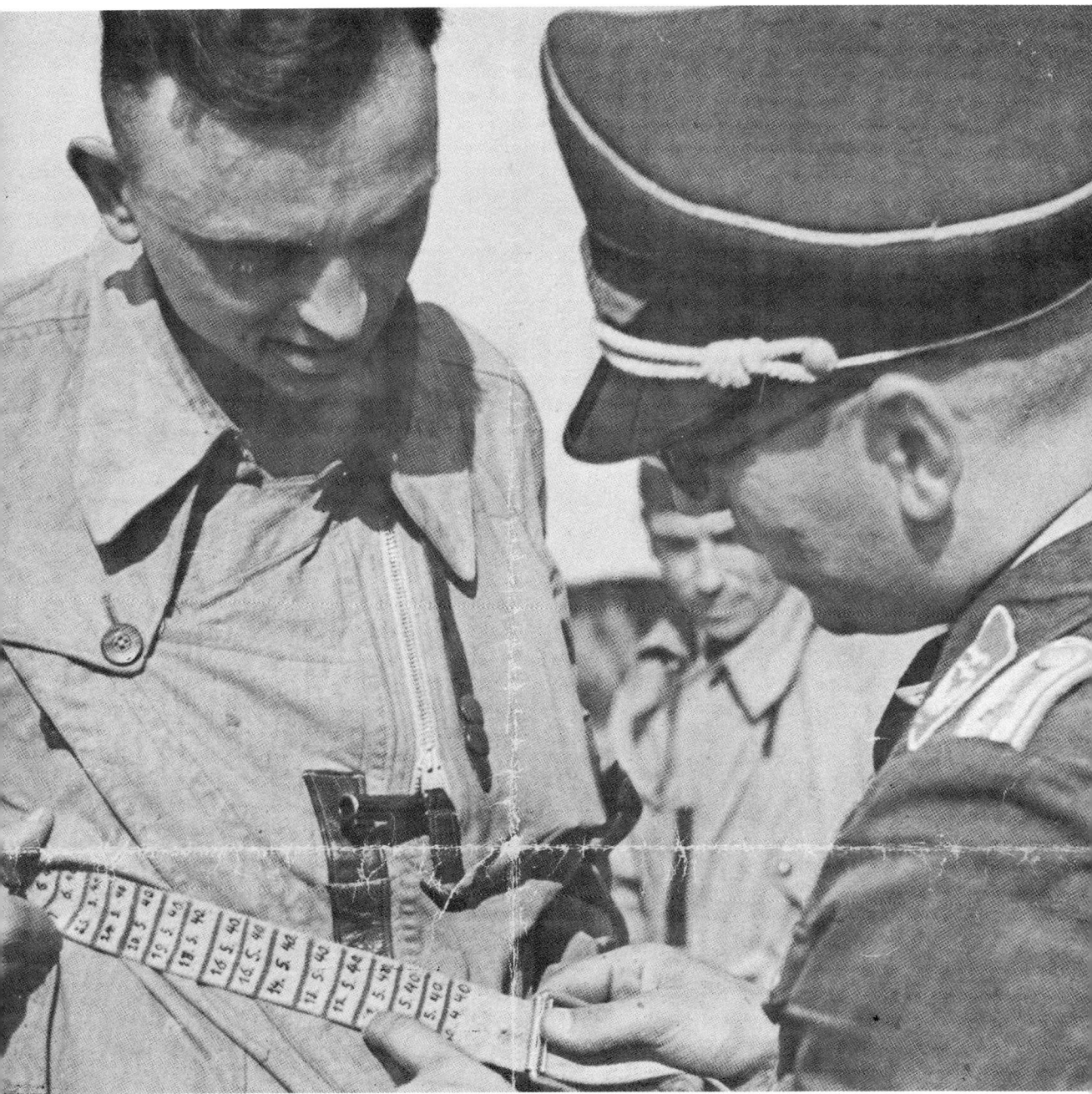

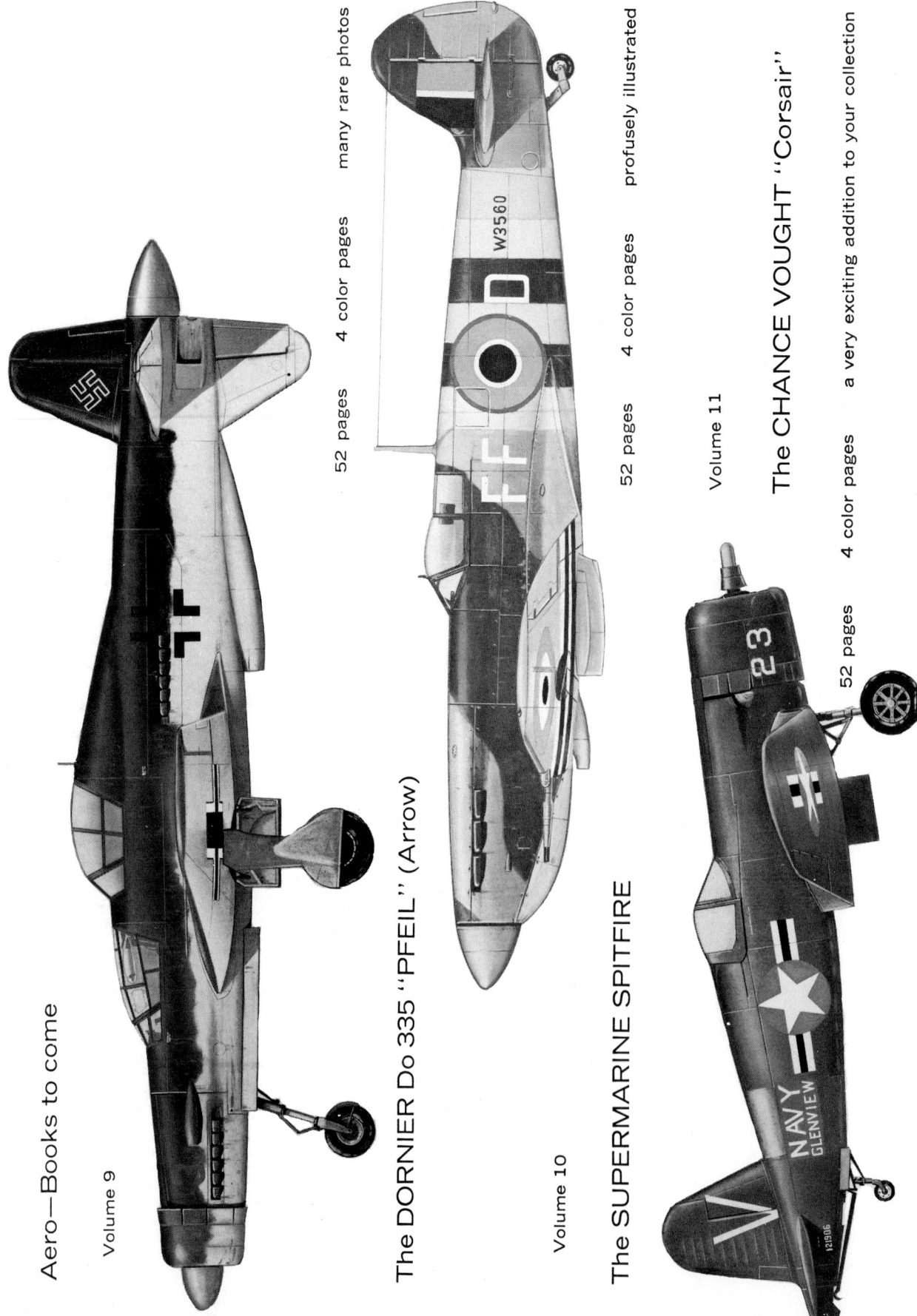

Aero—Books to come

Volume 9

The DORNIER Do 335 "PFEIL" (Arrow)  52 pages  4 color pages  many rare photos

Volume 10

The SUPERMARINE SPITFIRE  52 pages  4 color pages  profusely illustrated

Volume 11

The CHANCE VOUGHT "Corsair"  52 pages  4 color pages  a very exciting addition to your collection